Dumped!

Helen Chapman

Series consultant: Lorraine Petersen

RISING STARS

NASEN House, 4/5 Amber Business Village, Amber Close, Amington,
Tamworth, Staffordshire B77 4RP

Rising Stars UK Ltd.
7 Hatchers Mews,
Bermondsey Street,
London SE1 3GS
www.risingstars-uk.com

Text © Rising Stars UK Ltd.

The right of Helen Chapman to be identified as the author of this work has been asserted by her in accordance with the Copyright, Design and Patents Act 1998.

Published 2009
Reprinted 2012, 2013

Cover design: Burville-Riley Partnership
Illustrator: Dave Neale for Advocate Art
Text design and typesetting: Andy Wilson for Green Desert Ltd.
Publisher: Gill Budgell
Editor: Catherine Gilhooly
Series consultant: Lorraine Petersen

All rights reserved. No part of this publication may be reproduced, stored in a retrieval system, or transmitted in any form by any means, electronic, mechanical, photocopying, recording or otherwise without the prior permission of Rising Stars UK Ltd.

British Library Cataloguing in Publication Data.
A CIP record for this book is available from the British Library

ISBN   978-1-84680-498-4

Printed by Craft Print International Limited, Singapore

Contents

Characters	4
Scene 1: Dumped!	7
Scene 2: Tricked!	17
Scene 3: Mugged!	28
Scene 4: Sorted!	38
In the chatroom ...	46

CHARACTERS

Kevin
Kevin is the eldest of three brothers. He can be a bit selfish.

Will
Will is the middle brother. He often gangs up with Kevin against their youngest brother Max.

Max
Max is the youngest brother and the peace maker.

Characters

Becca
Becca is a cousin of the boys. She is like Kevin and Will, but she doesn't see this in herself.

Lily
Lily is Becca's younger sister. She is practical and sensible.

Narrator
The narrator tells the story.

Scene 1
DUMPED!

Narrator Kevin, Will and Max are not happy. They've been kicked out of their home and are off to stay with their granny.

Will It's all Dad's fault.

Kevin Yeah. Just because he can't pay the rent doesn't mean we should suffer.

Will He could have got a second job.

Kevin Or worked nights.

Max You guys could get weekend jobs.

Dumped!

Will Good one, Max. And what about my football matches?

Kevin As if my basketball team could win without me.

Will It's okay for Dad. He gets to move in with his mate Terry.

Kevin Yeah, why can't we do that?

Max Because you hate Terry.

Kevin So? He doesn't know that.

Max You called him dog-breath to his face.

Narrator He did too. But in fairness to Kevin, Terry isn't big on using a toothbrush!

Kevin Will is right.

Will Am I? What about?

Kevin About moving in with a mate. We're not allowed to.

Scene 1   Dumped!

Max   Terry lives close to Dad's work. Dad will save loads of money by not having to catch the train every day.

Will   Nah, he just doesn't want to live with Granny.

Narrator   Across town, sisters Lily and Becca come out of the train station. They're having much the same chat as the boys.

Lily   I can't believe we've been kicked out of home.

Becca   It's all Mum's fault. She's so selfish.

Lily   I know! She gets to go on a business trip overseas and we get to suffer.

Becca   Having to stay with Granny for a whole month!

Dumped!

Lily: At least Mum didn't make us go and stay with those awful cousins of ours.

Narrator: Both girls shudder.

Becca: Urghh! Don't even joke about it! I bet they're still not house-trained.

Narrator: As the girls walk to Granny's house, a bus pulls up. Some boys charge out and push past them.

Becca: Hey! Watch it!

Lily: Who let you apes loose?

Becca: Yeah, does the zoo know you've escaped?

Narrator: The boys turn around to face the girls. Then the cousins all recognise each other.

Will: Don't start! We are *not* having a good day.

Scene 1   Dumped!

Max I am. Hi Lily. Hi Becca.
You don't live around here, do you?

Lily Not likely.

Becca We're going to Granny's place.

Max Cool! Just like Red Riding Hood.

Kevin So are we.

Max What? Like Red Riding Hood?

Kevin No. Going to Granny's.

Lily How come? You won't get any money – it's not Christmas!

Will and Kevin (*together*)
We've been dumped!

Dumped!

Becca What do you mean?

Max We've got to live with Granny until Dad finds us somewhere cheap to live.

Becca What? You mean *you're* staying with Granny?

Lily But you can't!

Max Watch us!

Will Anyway, what's it got to do with you?

Lily A lot. We're staying there too.

Kevin You can't be. She must have confused you with us.

Becca That's *so* wrong in *so* many ways.

Lily Mum told Granny weeks ago that we were staying.

Narrator She did too!

Scene 1   Dumped!

Max   Well, Dad told Granny weeks ago that we were staying.

Narrator   He did too!

Becca   I bet she forgot about you. It's easy to do.

Narrator   Who are they again?

Kevin   Look. How are we going to sort this?

Will   It's easy. The girls all share Granny's room.

Kevin   So you and I get a room each. Works for me.

Max   And what about me?

Kevin   Ask someone who cares.

Lily   Well, that's it then, is it? You've sorted it all.

Will   Works for me.

Dumped!

Narrator Becca grabs her sister's arm
and whispers.

Becca Walk with me. Quickly.

Lily Why?

Becca Because if we get there first ...
then we'll get our pick of the rooms.

Lily Oh right. Cool.

Narrator But the boys aren't as dumb
as the girls think. Well, at least
one of them isn't.

Max Why are Lily and Becca running off?

Will Girl stuff.

Max What?

Kevin You know. Girls. Bathrooms.
They always go in pairs.

Scene 1   Dumped!

Max   You don't think they might be trying to get to Granny's first?

Will   For what?

Max   The best bedroom.

Kevin   They wouldn't dare.
             Anyway, I'm Granny's favourite.

Narrator   Even Kevin isn't sure that's true!

Max   How are we going to make this work?

Will   It's easy. Like I said, the girls can share with Granny.

Kevin   So you and I get a room each. Works for me.

Will   And me.

Max   What about me?
             You always forget about me.

Dumped!

Kevin So? You're easy to forget.

Will I know. We can put you in the shed.

Kevin You mean the one Granny always keeps locked?

Will Yeah, it'd be perfect for Max.

Max I'm out of here. You coming?

Kevin Why waste the effort? I'm the oldest. The best room is mine.

Narrator Will gives him an icy smile.

Will You mean *ours* don't you?

Kevin Yeah, yeah. Just kidding.

Scene 2

TRICKED!

Narrator Max races into Granny's house. He trips over a black glove with a long cuff.

Max What's Granny doing with this? It looks like something a knight might wear.

Kevin Don't mind me.

Will Or me.

Narrator Kevin and Will push past Max and look for the girls.

Lily Granny's bed is *so* comfy, isn't it Becca?

Dumped!

Becca   Yep. Soooo big and soooo comfy.

Narrator   Will and Kevin rush into Granny's room.

Will   You're dreaming if you think
you're keeping this room.

Kevin   Yeah, if it's the best room it's mine …

Will   *Ours.*

Kevin   So get out!

Narrator   The girls leave but talk loudly
so the boys can hear every word.

Becca   Losers! They think that's the best room.

Lily   Maybe they like wallpaper
with flowers on.

Becca   I'd just die if my
friends saw me in it.

Scene 2   Tricked!

Lily   Quick. We'll take the back bedroom.
             It's wicked!

Becca   Yeah and it's away from Granny's room,
             so we can be noisy.

Narrator The boys are confused.
             More than usual!

Max   That back room sounds better
             than this one.

Kevin   I'm not backing down.
             They'll think I'm a loser.

Will   We'll all be losers if we take this room.
             Can it have any more flowers?

Max   It looks nice …

Narrator Kevin and Will turn to look at Max.

Max   … you know … if you're a granny.

Dumped!

Will   I'll never live it down
if I bring mates back.

Kevin   You're right.
We'll all be laughed out of school.
Lily, Becca, get back here.

Lily   What's up?

Kevin   We don't want this room anymore
because ... um ... er ...

Will   Because ... um ... er ...

Lily   Okay. Okay. We give in.
But this is the last time we move.
Got it?

Kevin   Yeah, yeah. We get it.

Scene 2   Tricked!

Narrator   The boys check out the back room.
They get a nasty shock. Two beds
are pressed against each wall,
with a fold-out bed squeezed
in the middle.

Kevin   You've got to be kidding!

Max   I'm not sleeping on that thing.

Will   Nah, it's good. If I roll out of bed
I'll land on something soft.

Max   Well, it's not going to be me!

Kevin   We were conned big time.
We'll have to pretend we like our room
or we'll look stupid.

Narrator   The girls squeeze into the room.

Becca   Like your room, boys?

Kevin   Yeah. It's like being at a sports camp.

Will   Bare floorboards are cool.
We can bounce balls off them.

Dumped!

Max And there's nothing to knock over
and get broken.

Kevin We're going to unpack
and get ready for school tomorrow.

Lily Do you have to change schools now
that you've moved away?

Will Nah, Dad sorted it.

Becca And it's not like you're here forever,
is it?

Narrator The boys shrug.

Kevin Hope not. School's so far away,
it's not funny.

Max But when we get back here
it'll be good.

Kevin We'll chill out and Granny
will do granny stuff,
like making us snacks.

Scene 2   Tricked!

Becca   Yeah, it's not as if she has her own life.

Narrator   The next day after school, the girls
are amazed to see the boys
sitting at the kitchen table
doing homework.

Lily   Why's it so quiet?

Max   Granny says no music.

Becca   I don't blame her.
We heard you singing in the shower.

Will   She took the radio.
She said we'd get it back
when we've done our homework.

Narrator   The girls grab a snack and go
into the living room. Then they
go back to the boys.

Becca   Have you seen anything missing?

Max   Like what?

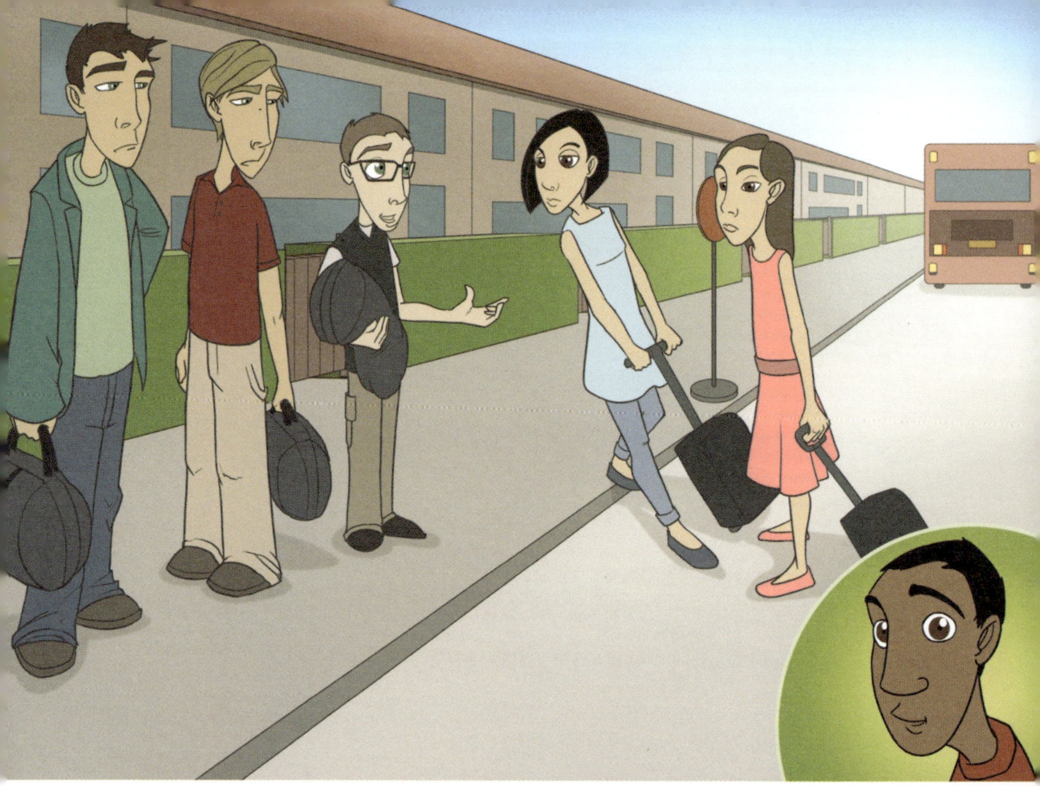

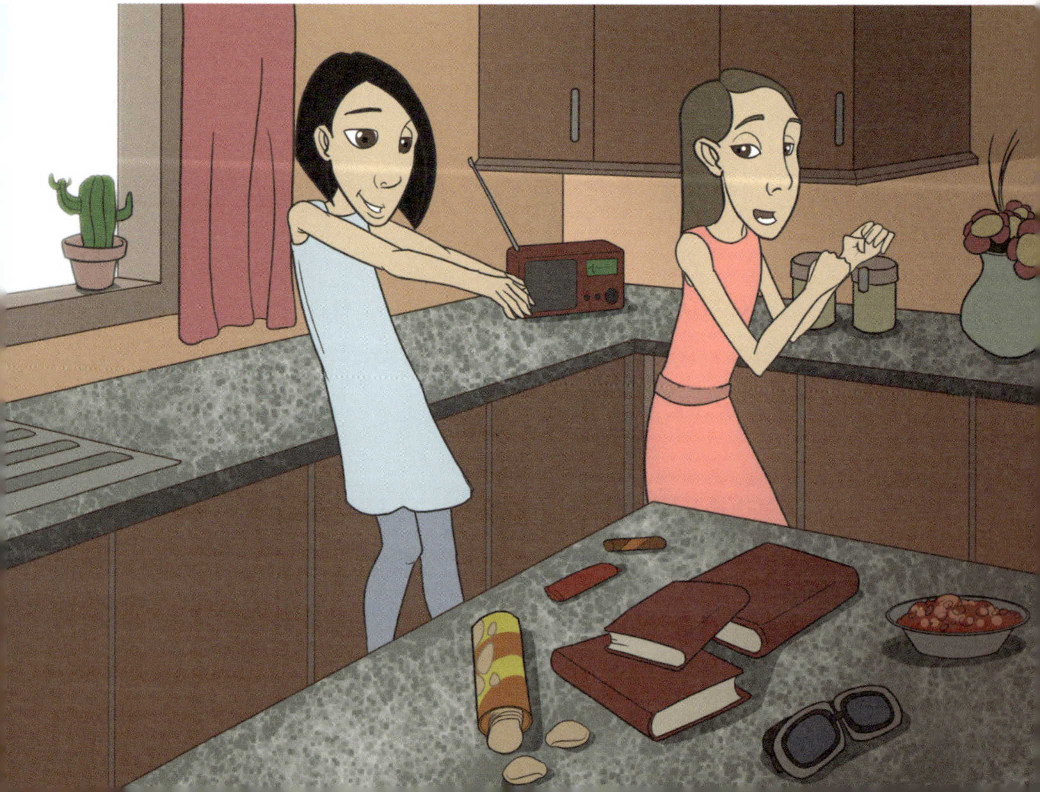

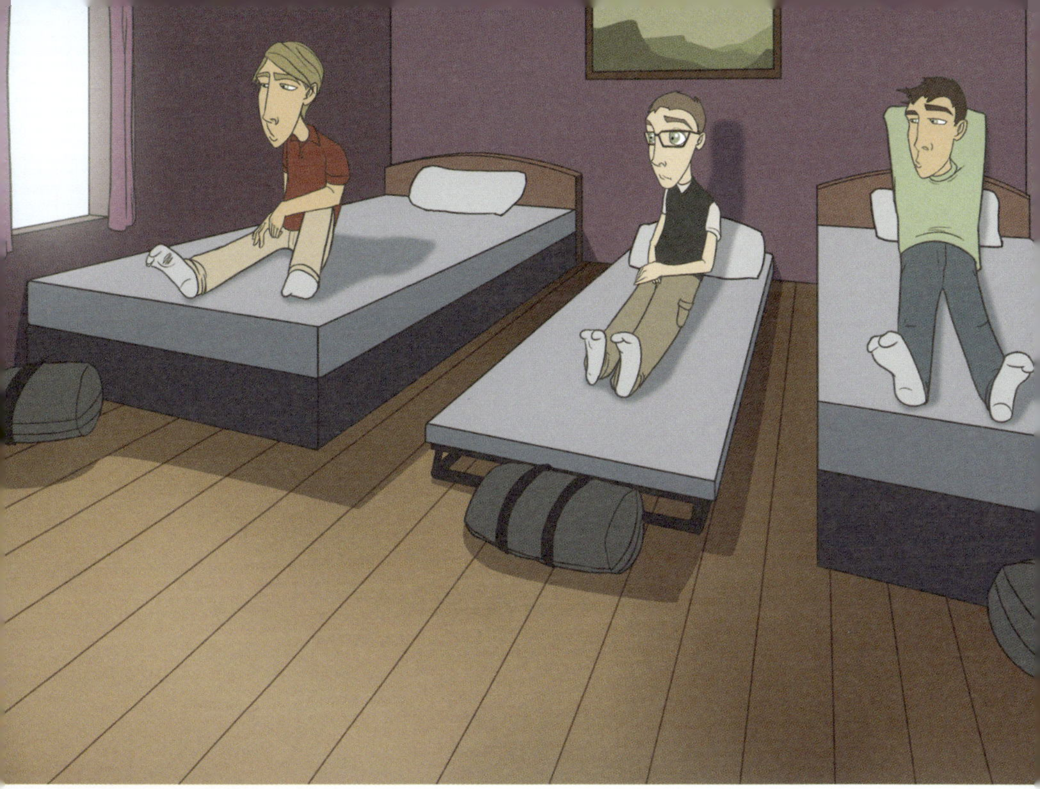

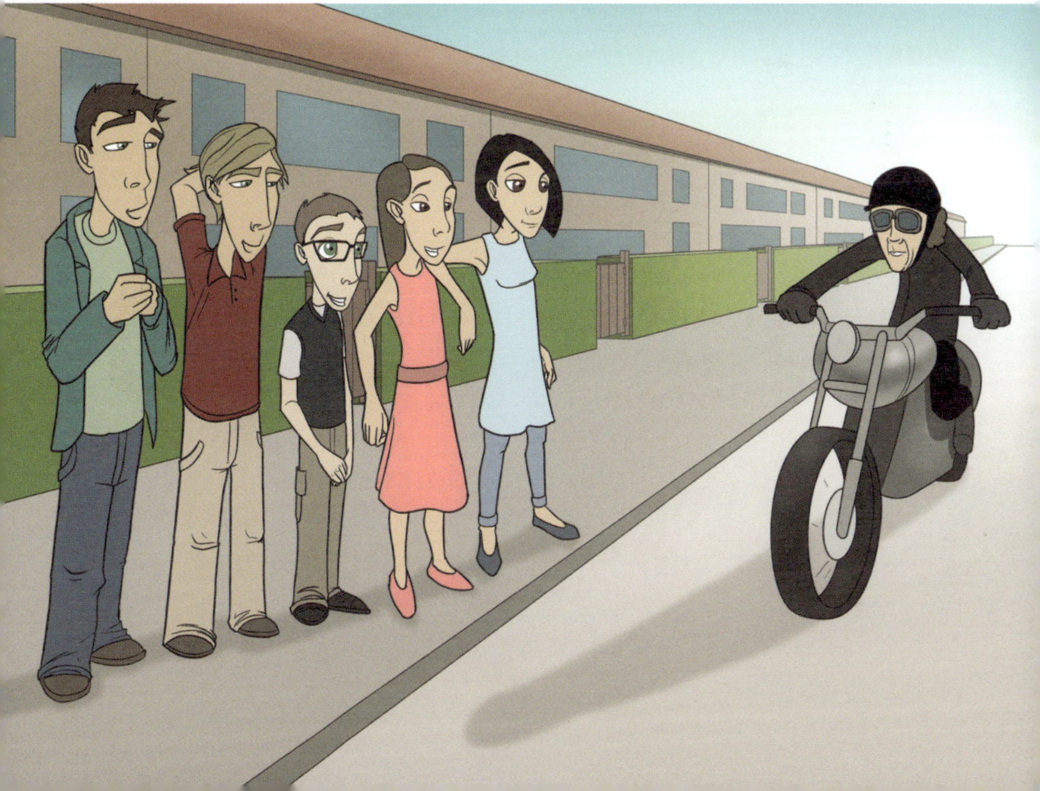

Dumped!

Lily   Get in here and look around.

Narrator   The boys shuffle into the living room.

Becca   The TV's gone.

Will   It's in Granny's room.

Kevin   Granny came home and found us watching it.

Will   Before she found us listening to the radio!

Max   From now on there's no TV on a school night.

Will   And we can't even watch TV over dinner.

Kevin   She's making us sit at the table.

Lily   And do what?

Max   Talk about how our day was.

Becca   How long does it take to say 'boring'?

Scene 2 Tricked!

Narrator Later that night the house is quiet and the cousins are asleep.
At least that's what Granny thinks.

Kevin It's half past nine! And I'm in bed! With the light out!

Max We're *all* in bed.

Kevin But I'm the oldest.
I never go to bed before eleven.

Will You do now. Granny's house. Granny's rules.

Kevin Not for much longer.

Max Why, what are you planning?

Kevin From now on, it's going to be *my* house, *my* rules.

Scene 3

MUGGED!

Narrator	By next Thursday afternoon, it's clear that Granny hasn't heard about Kevin being in charge.
Lily	Kevin! What are you doing here? You said you'd be at basketball practice.
Kevin	I couldn't go. There was no way to get home.
Will	Same for me and football.
Max	And for me and Scouts.

Scene 3   Mugged!

Lily	Ever heard of a bus?
Becca	Or train?
Will	Granny won't let us.
Lily	You're joking, right?
Max	No. She's worried about us getting mugged.
Becca	Couldn't you get a lift?
Will	No one from school lives around here.
Kevin	Anyway. Back to me. What am I going to do about training?
Will	Just go. We'll take turns to cover for each other.
Lily	That won't work. Granny's home when we are.
Kevin	She really spoils our fun, doesn't she?
Lily	A bit, but I like her being here when I get home.

Dumped!

Will   I don't. I like being home alone.
           You get away with stuff.

Max   Dad never got back before meal time.
           I never used to start my homework
           until eight.

Will   And Dad never told me
           to get my muddy boots off the bed.

Narrator I bet he did.

Kevin   And he let me chill out and do nothing.

Narrator I bet he didn't.

Max   Granny doesn't believe in chilling out.

Kevin   Tell me about it. She always finds
           something for us to do.

Will   Like putting out the rubbish.

Lily   You three are unreal.
           Stop and think about Granny.

Scene 3 Mugged!

Becca She had this place to herself.
Now she has five kids to look after.

Will We look after ourselves at home.

Becca No you don't. Your dad
juggles work with looking after you.

Max How do you know?

Lily I've heard my mum and your dad talking.

Will So go on then, what does he say?

Lily That you three are selfish,
lazy and messy.

Kevin What? No way!

Lily Kevin, who always picked you up
from basketball?

Kevin Dad.

Becca Will, who picked you up
from football?

Will Dad.

Lily   Max, who picked you up from Scouts?

Max   Dad.

Kevin   I see where you're going with this.

Narrator   Kevin's quick off the mark, isn't he?

Kevin   You think Granny should drive us.

Lily   No! I'm saying that you should look after yourself more.

Will   We're okay with meeting up and coming home together.

Max   It's Granny who's scared for us.

Kevin   Will you help us?

Becca   To do what?

Kevin   Get Granny to pick me up from basketball.

Will   And me from football.

Scene 3   Mugged!

Max   And me from Scouts.

Becca   What's in it for us?

Kevin   You get rid of us
            every Thursday afternoon.

Becca   Anything that keeps you out of
            the house sounds good.

Lily   We'll tell Granny you miss your dad
            and you'd like her to watch you train.

Narrator   The plan works! The next Thursday afternoon the girls turn their music up loud and dance around the house.

Dumped!

Becca   Quick! Before Granny gets back, let's spread our homework out on the table.

Lily   Hey! Whose black leather goggles are these?

Becca   No idea. I'll turn off the music.

Narrator   They needn't have bothered. Granny storms down the side path and into the shed.

Lily   What's up with her?

Max   Granny was mugged!

Lily and Becca (*together*)
    Mugged?!

Kevin   Her bag was snatched, but she wasn't hurt.

Becca   What happened?

Scene 3   Mugged!

Max   Granny picked me and Will up.
Then we went to get Kevin.

Will   But he was still training,
so we watched and ...

Kevin   I was awesome if you're wondering.

Lily and Becca (*together*)
We're not!

Will   These kids ran into us ...

Max   ... and grabbed Granny's purse.

Will   Granny pulled out a spanner ...

Lily   What spanner?

Will   The one in her bag.

Becca   Granny carries a spanner in her bag?

Narrator   Mine carries a bus pass!

Will   Granny chased them
and they dropped her purse.

Dumped!

Becca So, she got everything back?

Kevin Yeah. She was awesome.

Becca So, why is she out in the shed?

Max To let off steam I guess.

Will You should have heard her in the car.
She went on and on about gangs.

Kevin And how they're taking over the streets.

Lily So, what happens next Thursday?

Becca We like having one afternoon
to ourselves.

Kevin If I can't train I'm off the team.

Will And if I can't train
I won't make the team!

Max And I need to train more
or I won't get my next Scouts badge.

Kevin There's more. We have to stay in
on the weekends.

Scene 3 Mugged!

Will Granny's scared the gang will try to get us back.

Narrator They're going to have to do something.

Max We've got to do something.

Narrator See, I told you.

Becca We'll talk to Granny.
Leave it with us.

Kevin No, we'll sort it.
This needs manpower.
Right?

Narrator Right!

Scene 4
SORTED!

Narrator	On Saturday the girls come down for breakfast.
Lily	Well, any ideas boys?
Narrator	Max shakes raisins covered in chocolate into the girls' hands.
Max	Throw them around the kitchen. We've done the rest of the house.
Becca	Why?

Scene 4   Sorted!

Max   Granny will think it's rat poo.
She'll call in pest control.

Kevin   They'll spray horrible stuff around
and we'll have to go out for the day.

Narrator   Just as the girls finish,
Granny comes downstairs.

Kevin   Everyone hide. Max, you keep watch.

Narrator   They hide, but the plan fails.

Max   It didn't work! Granny just picked up the
raisins and told us to stop making a mess!

Narrator   Becca turns to Kevin.

Becca   Is there a chance that you and Will
will think of something sensible?

Narrator   I don't think so.

Dumped!

Kevin   We set a trap up last night.

Narrator   They walk into the hallway and Kevin shows them lots of hidden bits of string.

Kevin   When Granny walks along here to get her post, she'll step on this string.

Will   It'll pull on the other bits of string and then pull on the door knocker.

Becca   And?

Max   She'll think someone's knocking and she'll open the door.

Becca   And?

Kevin   Nobody will be there but she'll say, "What a lovely day. I think I'll go into town and do whatever it is old people do."

Lily   You guys aren't apes, you're morons.

Kevin   I can't see anything *you've* done.

Scene 4 Sorted!

Lily That's because there's nothing to see.

Will Huh?

Becca We've sorted it out by thinking smart.

Kevin As if!

Lily We asked Granny if she'd be home today.

Becca She said something about cycling to meet something.

Will And you let us do all this stuff for nothing?

Becca Not for nothing. We wanted to see this manpower of yours!

Narrator An engine revs. But they're too busy arguing to notice.

Kevin The moment Granny goes, then I'm off.

Lily But Granny said we should stay here.

Dumped!

Will She never made us promise.

Kevin We'll go into town.

Becca I'm staying.

Max What are you going to do?

Becca Find out what's in the shed.

Lily Good idea. I've wanted to see inside the shed ever since I was little.

Max Me too. None of us has ever been allowed in there.

Will Where does Granny hide the spare key?

Lily Who knows? Let's start looking.

Kevin I'll see you later. Will, are you coming?

Will Yes. But I'll help look for the key when I get back.

Narrator They look for two hours. The key's not on shelves, not under cans of food, and not under Sid, the garden gnome!

Scene 4 Sorted!

Becca I've found it!

Lily Where?

Becca On a hook by the back door.

Max Cool! I'd never have looked there.

Lily Let's check out the shed before Granny gets back.

Narrator Becca fits the key into the lock on the shed. But they all jump when they hear the back door slam open.

Max Its okay. It's only Kevin and Will.

Will Guess who we saw?

Lily That gang?

Kevin Worse. Granny!

Becca Oh no! Did she see you?

Will Hard to tell ... she was going so fast.

Dumped!

Lily But her car's in the garage.
We saw it when we looked for the key.

Kevin Get this. She was on a Harley!

Becca What's a Harley?

Will Only an awesome motor cycle.

Max Oh, so that explains the glove
and the spanner ...

Lily And the goggles.

Narrator Becca opens the shed door.
Inside they see a tool kit,
spare motor cycle parts and a small
motor cycle.

Will Wow!

Kevin Do you think Granny will teach us
to ride?

Becca We can save our pocket money
and buy a helmet.

Scene 4   Sorted!

Lily   And goggles and gloves.

Narrator   They hear the roar of an engine coming closer.

Will   That's Granny now. We'll go and meet her.

Becca   I'll lock the door and put the key back.

Max   I hope she never finds out.

Kevin   Yeah, she might dump us right back home before we learn to ride.

Narrator   But although Granny was tempted – she didn't!

In the chatroom ...

You read this message posted by Max in an online chatroom.

Message posted by
Max

Sat 11.15 a.m.

Family trouble: Any ideas?

I'm living at my granny's house with my older brothers. Granny has loads of house rules – and my brothers just don't agree with them. I kinda like living at Granny's and I don't want to upset her. How do I make my brothers see that they should stick to her rules?

- Write an email to Max giving him some ideas. (Maybe he could ask his cousins to help him?)

Role play ...

- Work with a partner. One person is Granny and the other person is one of the children.
- The child has to try to convince Granny that they should be allowed to watch TV and listen to music whenever they like.
- Granny has to explain her reasons against this, e.g. they need to do their homework in a quiet place, at dinner time it's nice to talk to your family instead of watching TV, etc.
- Can both sides come to an agreement?

Find the clues ...

- *Work with a partner. Pretend you are super detectives! Look back through the play and see if you can find the clues about Granny's secret hobby.*
- *Talk with your partner about how you felt when you found out about Granny's motor cycle. Were you surprised?*
- *Say whether you think it was a good ending or not, and why.*

INTERACT

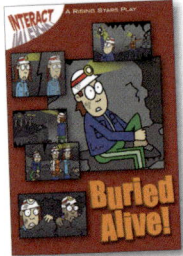

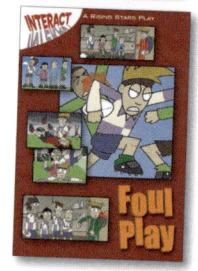

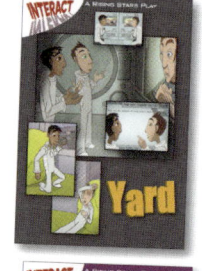

ASTRO-MAN

TOFFEE NOSE

BURIED ALIVE!

FOUL PLAY

PLANE CRAZY

YARD

DUMPED!

STEP WARS

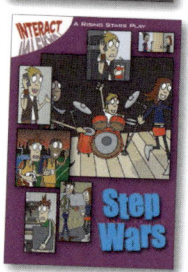

Interact plays are available from booksellers or
www.risingstars-uk.com

For more information please call freephone 0800 091 1602

RISING ★ STARS